Black Girl Lost

— A Survivor's Testimony —

MARIE ALI

AuthorHouse™
1663 Liberty Drive
Bloomington, IN 47403
www.authorhouse.com
Phone: 1 (800) 839-8640

Published by AuthorHouse 01/03/2019

ISBN: 978-1-5462-7423-0 (sc)
ISBN: 978-1-5462-7422-3 (e)

Library of Congress Control Number: 2018915292

Print information available on the last page.

Any people depicted in stock imagery provided by Getty Images are models,
and such images are being used for illustrative purposes only.
Certain stock imagery © Getty Images.

This book is printed on acid-free paper.

Because of the dynamic nature of the Internet, any web addresses or links contained in this book may have changed
since publication and may no longer be valid. The views expressed in this work are solely those of the author and do
not necessarily reflect the views of the publisher, and the publisher hereby disclaims any responsibility for them.

authorHOUSE®

This book is dedicated to my grandmother. No matter what my circumstances are your door has always been open to me. I have battled myself but you assured me that I did not need to, that we all go through trials and tribulations. I was a Black Girl Lost but I am now a Black Woman found. Thank you grandma, the alchemist, the matriarch, the queen, my heart.

The Foundation

What woman is one dimensional? Are there any more complex beings on this earth than females? We can create life and nurture it. We are the queens of the earth, the protector of mankind. A woman possesses the true power that men think they do. We do not do one thing. We do many things well. I am not just a woman. I am not just a writer. I hurt. I love. I frown and I smile. I party and I pray. The names have been changed but the pain remains the same. I am a whole and these are the pieces of me. This is my story, the story of a Black girl lost that is now found.

CHAPTER 1

Roots

Where we come from doesn't necessarily determine who we will be.

How we are loved determines everything. Today, marriage and having children are taken so lightly. The commitment does not mean what it once used to. Men treat women as throw away items, a tool to be used and their children suffer as a result. The black race is dying because we no longer have a strong family foundation. Drugs, violence, affairs, abuse, mental illness and alcohol tear apart our homes from the ground floor to the roof. Children see and experience way too much way too soon. It has always been beyond me why we then feel the need to add to that. My experiences on this earth have been traumatizing but thanks to God I have been able to triumph. What happens to those who aren't quite so lucky? None of us ask to be here and when we are and the beginning of life is chaotic, what will be the end result? This is the important lesson we all must learn about having strong roots.

There were days my older brother and I would be too scared to even use the bathroom or play too loudly, for fear of making our mother angry. Just coming out of our rooms had the potential to be dangerous. I knew I had to be quick whether I wanted to grab toys or a sandwich. My brother was always there behind me to shield me from the senseless beatings. We recently laughed during a phone conversation about how we were almost ninjas in training, swinging from cabinets in order to not make too much noise to get something to eat. We were a dynamic duo, when I lost touch with him for years it was a devastating and unbearably sad time. Despite being so fortunate financially, we were lacking in one area, that area is love.

My parents married when I was 3 years old. I don't remember any of it but I did see the pictures and I saw how happy they once were. It is hard to believe all of that happiness would one day turn into so much pain and chaos. I wondered how pop's drinking and drugging started and if it really did numb all of the pain. I got to know alot about him when he released his book, "The Fullness of a Man" . I am still learning many things about him through his writing. Pops attempted suicide in December 2016 and my life would never be the same, but more about that later.

Pops was an alcoholic; I now know why he drank. Even then I never stopped loving him because he wasn't a mean drunk. He showed me, even though they weren't his kids, my older brother's love. They were all taught to fish, play football and just be happy young men. My oldest brother, Desmond just told me the story about how Pops bought him his first football and him and Cousin C ran into the yard to toss it around, elated to be with Pops and have a Black man that was not their father care so much about them. To some that may seem like a small gesture but young Black men do not have alot of guidance, kindness shown to them . I could tell the way his eyes lit up as he told me this anecdote and so many others that my Pops had an incredibly positive influence on his life. If I could re-write history I would have kept us all together, writing, playing music and being a loving, hard-working family until. The details are all pretty blurry from this stage of my life. I am not sure if that can be attributed to age or just trying to block out the trauma. I do remember that I was very quiet at this time in my life, didn't really speak as a reaction. In a way I had lost my voice before I even got a chance to really find it at all. I loved to sing in my room ; I would take my oldest brothers boom box and cassette tapes into the bathroom or the hall closet and pretend I was Janet Jackson, Madonna, Paula Abdul or whoever had a hit song on the radio at the time. I watched the Cosby Show on TV and wondered why my family couldn't be like that. After all, the actress Keisha Knight Pulliam and I share the same birthday so why couldn't I just have her life for a day? It all seemed so perfect and cookie cutter. There was never a conflict on that show that they could not solve as long as they came up with a solution together. They were a strong family unit with their parents and grandparents as the foundation; I wanted that more than anything.

My imagination became very vivid and active at this time. I would put on plays for my brothers and dress up and sing and dance all around the living room. My parents did not know what to do with my energy. I was wild and free and always had a huge smile on my face despite the pain that I felt inside. My smile started to fade over the years. Trauma and abuse took away the sparkle in my eyes and I am still fighting to get back what was taken from me. The beatings were so senseless and would come when we least expected it. My second oldest brother and I got the brunt of them as our oldest brother was now in a group home and we only saw him on the weekends. He was always in trouble for stealing or talking back.

The abuse was something I can never forget. Being slapped, kicked, punched, choked all because she was angry with one of our Pop's, about her job or just plain mad as hell. One day my father had enough of the arguing, fussing and fighting that was contributing to his spiraling into a web of addiction. Even now, looking at pictures from that time the only thing I could see on my father's face was pain. Pops left one day and I won't forgive him for it but I can try to understand the reasoning behind it because I was never really given one. I still struggle with what he and my mom went through had to do with me. What does it ever have to do with the children? Even to this day it is hard for me to trust men because of the fear that they will leave me one day with or without explanation. I believe psychologists call these abandonment issues.

CHAPTER 2

Perfect Stranger

My mother is what psychologists call co-dependent so she never missed a beat when it came to finding a man. I must tell you my life was fragile from the start; I was exposed to too many things too soon. When I was 1 years old, Mr. B came into my life. She had grown up with him in the projects of Yonkers, NY and from what I understand, he has always been trouble. She had actually dated his brother, damn did this lady make the wrong choice!! Most men bring out the best in their partner, this man brought out the absolute worst in my mom. Cheating, violence, emotional abuse, you name it, they went through it. At this stage of my life I knew that she could care less about me, not because it was voluntary but because some women resent their daughters and let's add in the factor that my mother suffers from mental illness. Now that I am older I am able to better comprehend how her illnesses being untreated and undertreated affected her parenting skills, therefore affected us all.

There were moments when we were all in such a state of shock that we couldn't believe that was our own mother allowing her children to be exposed to what we were. My mom loved to take her aggression out on us. She would get stressed from her job, sometimes jobs. She would feed us McDonald's, if we were lucky, otherwise we all had to learn to make cereal and other simple meals. This was early on. My youngest brother and I got 3 square meals a day but that was during the most traumatic years. We were never on the streets or in a foster home but sometimes I would pray that she would just leave us alone so that I could run away. For the most part we were latchkey kids. We did it all. If not, we learned to do it and fast. There was never a dull moment; life was always in limbo, full of drama for us to be so young; when I look back maybe that's the way that God intended it to be. Once my Pops left, we were all split apart. We moved back to New York and with that came a few revelations. Mom had a hell of a way of showing that she cared about us. She would come by my Aunt's house where we were staying and drop a couple of dollars, not enough to even feed us and some too small clothing and shoes. She was around us so little she did not even know our sizes. To this day this is why I love to keep up my clothes and shoes. I know how it feels to have that area of life neglected. Mr. B became my full-time babysitter. He was a smooth talking correction officer and mechanic on the side. He had me convinced he was the nicest guy in the world and that I could trust him. My grandmother told me that many people in her church knew of him as a young kid and he was never anything but trouble. I was unaware of how he would impact my life. I just thought I had a new dad, someone to fill the void of abandonment that my Pops had left. Life was supposed to be so simple when you were in elementary school. I made a lot of friends; it has always been an easy thing for me to do. I even had a couple of boys have crushes on me but I did not feel like I was worthy of such a thing. One of those crushes is still my friend after 28 years. A quiet, Jamaican boy who seemed to think I was the greatest thing since sliced bread. His brothers would walk me to the library, they had no idea what they were helping me escape by sitting there for hours reading with me and doing their homework. To some degree, I can credit them all with helping me to become a writer. Reading and writing became my escape from life. My innocence had been lost so I frequently wondered what was so special about me. I was tarnished, who could admire that? The pain and shame turned to anger and I was so mean towards him and other boys that made advances towards me. It was all completely innocent but I could not distinguish them not wanting the same thing that was being forcibly taken from me at home. I did not have the mental capacity or rationale to decipher any of what was happening to me. I was a child who once again was forced to grow up way too soon. I even find it useless to try and explain it today. There is no way anyone can understand abuse unless they have lived through it themselves but I am glad it is more in conversation today. One day in school we learned about good touch and bad touch. I stayed behind in class and told the teacher I was getting bad touches at home. I even told the cab driver who drove me to school. He consulted his girlfriend and she told him the wrong thing. She told him to talk to Mitzy. The gates of hell may as well have opened as far as I was concerned. The school called mom and she told them I lied a lot and that night I got the beating of my life. She told me not to be fresh around her new husband with a certain tone that told me she knew what was happening, may have even had a part in it. I refused to truly think my Mitzy was that damn crazy until one night I awoke to him touching me and she was there in the doorway watching. He began raping me once I developed breasts. I got used to being attacked, especially at night. Sometimes I was getting raped three times a day while she was at work or shopping or something. She seemed to never be home, there is no way that was just a coincidence. It hurt more emotionally than physically. He used to try and video tape me in the shower, claimed he was trying to record me singing. I kept journals for years about the abuse. My Mitzy found them one day after I had left home and destroyed them. My story would have been a lot easier to tell if I still had them. I can never bring myself back to that place to remember how I felt. All I know is I could never go back and go through it all again. By 16, I was a mess. I was making myself throw up from the stress of the abuse. The bathroom was my escape, binging and purging I was able to release the pain even if it was temporary. At least it made me feel something and I had control over what was otherwise a chaotic life. I was embarrassed and ashamed about having a "white girl's disease". Bulimia was my life, all I could think about was going food shopping after school so that I could go home and purge. I was a dancer for 12 years and played high school basketball so my physique did not alarm anyone. I was a challenge to Mr. B by then though. I threatened him physically and with force. The headspace that my disease had me in did not allow me to have any fear because I no longer had any rationale. I also told him I would tell my Pops and he never touched me again. Looking back, I wish I would have just called my Pops and told him what was happening. I guess it was a trial I had to go through so that I could help young girls who go through the same things. Mitzy was only for herself so I know that she wouldn't help me, especially through an eating disorder. By the time I was 18, I was in therapy but she threatened me never to tell anyone this was happening in our home or she would have to move away. She doesn't even know to this day that I am a recovering Bulimic, how the abuse from my stepfather caused so much pain that I nearly killed myself purging. How she could be a mother and that be her main concern is beyond me and to this day I believe she is still in denial about the whole thing. I'm not, I lived it and I deal in reality not a dream world of what I think people believe my life should be. I hid my private pain from everyone but my dance teacher. She knew I struggled but I don't think she knew the extent of it. She moved her dance studio and left town without a trace one day. I am not sure if it was because she couldn't help me or if it was personal but I no longer had my outlet. I couldn't express myself and beat my pain into the dance floor. I realized soon after that just like the old days I had to learn how to help myself. Mr. B did not win. He thinks he did and he thinks he got away with it but I believe there is a special place in hell for him. I can no longer send him to jail for what he did, time ran out on that when I was 23 and I was just not strong enough to go through a trial. God will seek his vengeance and everything he did to me will come back to him. I do not wish harm on anyone but what he took from me can never be replaced. I hate him for what he did, who he made me become.

In 2005 I met Liza during treatment at a world-renowned facility for eating disorder recovery. She suffered from anorexia and bulimia and was also a survivor of childhood sexual abuse. She told me her story through her art work. To this day I think it should be hanging in a gallery somewhere. I told her my story through writing poetry. We shared our pain and artistry for 4 long weeks. Last summer, 2011 I learned that Liza never got a hold of her bulimia and died of heart failure at 28 years old. I cried for her, I cried for myself, I cried for all the girls and women who suffer sexual assault and abuse and punish themselves rather than heal. I look at all the celebrities who come out with stories of childhood sexual abuse.

From Oprah to Tyler Perry, Maya Angelou and Monique. So many deal with this pain and so many choose to keep silent. Telling your story is nothing to be ashamed or embarrassed about. It helps to heal to give your testimony as any good church-going person knows. You are the victim but you don't have to live like that for the rest of your life! Get back your power and let your attacker (s) know that they did not win! Mine may not be sitting in a jail cell but you can rest assure that God has the ultimate vengeance planned for him. It is not only for you but it can heal others too ; those who are going through it and have no one to tell. Or are too afraid to tell but you can be their ears. I've gotten many girls out of life threatening situations just by telling them my story in support groups, churches, and of course in my writing. I started to paint again this summer and I will always think about my friend and how she changed me.

CHAPTER 4

Breakdown

I had suffered for eight years at the hand of my stepfather. I found it difficult to get through most days without breaking down and crying. One day, I got the worst news of all; Mitzy and Mr. B were getting married.

She asked me how I felt and then told me that he would be my new Pops. "What the hell?! "Is what I was thinking but I was not yet outspoken at this stage of my life so I said nothing. He was a source of strength in her eyes; a new provider, someone who could make her look good. She would come off to the world as a mother who did for her kids including get with a guy who would be a good dad for them. We as her children and family, however, knew the real deal. Mr. B had been around since I was about 1 years old off and on but it wasn't until they started dating that my life would be forever changed. There were moments when I had suicidal thoughts. I couldn't take being violated, crying and having my voice fall on deaf ears. I was alone in the world, I was suffering in silence. By the age of 13, I was majorly depressed and keeping a journal about how much I hated Mitzy and Mr. B. I wanted to disappear and I wanted the pain to go away. I started taking an interest in boys around then and blocked out the trauma by being the class clown. The more school dances I attended and pickup basketball games I played, the better I started to feel about myself. This was also the year I changed school districts so I had a new batch of friends which was great. I saw it as a new group of people that I would have to hide my secret from. I was on the typical teenage journey through self-discovery and boy was it a journey. I experienced the pain of puberty while getting violated even more because I now had breasts. At this point I was happy outside my home but lived in a shroud of darkness that others would call a home.

I was a dreamer and storyteller so I wrote the most prolific essays in school. One teacher told me that she had never seen someone so young write with so much pain, If only she knew. I was a great fighter but at the same time I was getting tired of the fight. Emotionally I was always drained from putting up the façade of being happy at school. At home I was just miserable and I wasn't afraid to show it. I showed my disdain by blasting MTV and hiding out in my room with snacks and my homework. I had no regard for anyone in the house except for my nine year old brother. He was my safe haven, someone I could confide in even though I was shielding him from the trauma. I never let him see me down, would always joke around with him or help him with his homework. I was the ultimate big sister although I was suffering greatly. Today, he is a wonderful father and husband. We seemed to have completely different childhoods even though we grew up in the same home. I am thankful that he did not experience a lot of the horrors that I did because he is everything to me and I want nothing but happiness for him and for him to continue to thrive. When I could not handle life and went into hospitals he was always the first one to come looking for me. I know that our sibling bond has its rough patches but to me it is unbreakable and for that I am eternally grateful.

CHAPTER 5

Good Girl Gone Bad

Survivors of sexual assault usually go to one or two of the extremes when it comes to sexual activities and experiences. Girls and women tend to either become passive when it comes to sex, put it off completely or until they are married. On the other hand, women go into the dark world of the porn industry, prostitution, stripping or become extremely promiscuous. I had my own mix of experiences and fell into neither one of these extremes. I had always been open when it came to sex even before I became a victim of sexual abuse. Maybe it was because I was born in the early 1980's when images of Madonna in cone bras and Michael Jackson grabbing his crouch dominated my senses. Out of intense fear and endless insecurities I did not have sex at my own will until I was 20 years old. I felt empowered during sex liked the fact that at this point in my life I could control what happened. Never did I expect to ever become a victim again and lose that sense of control. I was raped in a mental institution while I was seeking treatment, y rape kit still sits in upstate NY with the millions of others, a symbol of the lack of urgency to attempt to rectify women's issues in this country. I had a lot of sex after this. I was not random with any of my selections, most of the men I had known for years, dated a few but I never expected them to want anything other than sex. I explored my sexuality with women, had threesomes, but I was always safe and always got tested for HIV and STD's, I may have been numbing my pain but I did not want to die. Everything and everyone in my path was a reason for me to become angry I often wondered if I can truly still consider myself a Christian after all of the lustful encounters I had. I know in my heart that I have been forgiven. God saw not just this part of my life, He saw the entire thing. We are not our circumstances but we surely react to them. Some will agree and some will not. At times it is hard to walk with my head held high but since recently losing 100 pounds I have a new found confidence in myself and the potential to be an even greater woman and positive example. I am not perfect, don't claim to be but I learned from my mistakes and that is more important than what anyone may feel about my actions or think about me. It is so easy to call a woman a hoe, slut, whore or many other colorful names. Most times we never take the time to figure out why she is like that or who might have hurt her to make her get to the point where she felt like she had no value and the only way to feel anything was to use her body for attention. It's time we stop judging and start listening.

CHAPTER 6

The Great Depression

There are two sides to every story, my childhood was bittersweet and it wasn't all traumatic. My mother was not an animal, does have a sweet side to her. I believe that's when she is consistent on medication and life is not stressing her out. She was the mom I wanted during these times, the mom I prayed for. During these times she wasn't Mitzy dearest at all. She would buy us toys, Christmases were always happy. That was just her putting up a front for the world though. That aspect has never changed. She was always worried about what "people would say or think". That's why my secret was never revealed until I became a woman. I lived in shame for eight years of my life, carrying guilt that should have been hers because she did not protect me as a mother should protect her children.

I was the mother to my youngest brother. All of my siblings and I were robbed of our childhood in the same ways the children were, if not worse, at times I felt like I just couldn't bear it anymore. I attempted suicide at the age of 13 and at the ages of 17, and 29. My mother was the most comforting when I was in the hospital with depression or an eating disorder issue. She seemed to be there the most when I was not well which made me feel that deep down she did have the capacity to nurture. The concept of me came early when she looked at my older cousin Rhea and wanted a girl. I was more of a plaything for her than a child; almost like a living doll. This led to her obsession with my weight and looks and why I ended up in units with bulimia and severe depression. I was a project; something that she could take care of. I would read and write a lot during these periods. Journal entries from when I was 15 and 16 would read like this: "*I think she is happy when I have relapses and breakdowns. It's fun for her! Her husband and her win when I have them but sometimes I just can't fight anymore. Life has thrown me so much. They have done so much sometimes I couldn't and still can't fight. I am getting sicker. The memories are making my binging and purging a daily thing. I want to tell my friends but I think they already know. I have to decide on a college, it's all too much. This is all I can control. I want to run from here! I will soon".* At this point in my life I had had enough. I put a stop to the sexual abuse; this landed me in a bad place when it should have been good. Emotionally I was a mess and physically I was damaging what once was an athletes and dancers body. I was down to 111 pounds. My mother hated me even more but pretended to love me in front of others. She was a secret abuser, like her husband. I was self-destructive. Life was suffocating me but I put on that famous smile for the world. I would keep it on as I entered my darkest depression since the age of 13.

"You have been accepted as an Honors scholar". These words were my escape. A chance to leave behind my personal hell for good was upon me and I felt excited for the first time in years. I got to campus that summer and I surprisingly experienced separation anxiety. Everything and everyone I had known was in New York. As painful as it all had been, I have no idea why I even looked back but I did. I started drinking to deal with the pain. My roommate was from New Jersey so we were a popular duo at the parties. I quickly jeopardized my scholarship by cutting class and sleeping through most of my dorm experience. I saw a counselor at school at my English professor's advisement and she quickly called the two people I could have waited a lifetime to see again. Mitzy and Mr. B drove back down to Maryland and promptly drove me to Grasslands hospital in Valhalla, NY. Seeing him caused severe emotional distress and I have to be tied to a gurney by three huge, black security guards. I was rolled onto a unit with men who were ogling my breasts through my thin hospital gown. Seconds later I was injected with thorozine, felt nothing for physically or emotionally for about 3 days. When I did come to, I was surrounded by visitors, two friends from high school who must have come from their campuses to see about me. Between the visits I played board games and stared at music videos with men

I didn't know and the nurses put my into an isolated room when one of them attempted to rape me in the community TV room. Again, my own mother left me in a vulnerable state. I began to cry for days on end. When she would come to visit Mitzy would just look at me and say "If you cry, they will never let you out of here". "Bitch, I hope they never do" was my only thought at that moment. The doctors told me Mr. B and Mitzy were afraid I would hurt them and were ordered to keep me under observation. My silence was again my own worst enemy. I would be in and out of 10 more hospitals for PTSD, Bulimia and depression for the rest of my 20's. I heard from a high school classmate a few years back that there was a rumor in my hometown that I "had gone crazy." I just wanted to make sure that the truth, my truth was told. There is no longer a need to wonder.

My life is now literally an open book.

At 18 I received a diagnosis of PTSD (Post Traumatic Stress Disorder) and anxiety disorder. PTSD would not become mainstream and most people would not know what an anxiety attack was until the following year after 9/11. The horrors I faced shaped how I react to everything and everyone. Had I not built up my defenses and found ways to protect myself I would not be alive to tell you my story today. I never compared myself or said that I had been through less or more than the average person. Most people don't talk about their lives in this much detail so there would be no way for me to know that for sure. I do know that a weaker person would not be able to handle all of this. I thank God for making me strong and for allowing me to be a survivor when I could have easily been a fatality. Depression affects so many of us. It knows no race, age, gender or name. I can only describe it as being eaten alive and spit back out. It is a staggering and debilitating illness. It is to be felt and learned from and one can never "snap out of it" but can learn to cope and live a happy and Fulfilling life.

Recent statistics suggest roughly seven of every one hundred people suffer depression after age 18 at some point in their lives.

- As many as one in 33 children and one in eight <u>adolescents</u> have clinicaldepression. Suicide is the third leading cause of death for ages 10 to 24.

- Most people diagnosed with major depression receive a diagnosis between their late twenties to mid-thirties.

- About six million people are affected by late life depression, but only 10% ever receive treatment.

- For every one man that develops depression, two women will, regardless of racial or ethnic background or economic status.

- More than half of all people caring for an older relative show clinically significant depressive symptoms.

- By the year 2020, depression will be the 2nd most common health problem in the world.

- **Getting Help**

- Here is the good news however: depression is one of the most treatable illnesses - 80-90% find relief. Researchers diligently work to develop new and successful treatments for depression among all age groups. Studies suggest patients that seek treatment, whether from <u>psychotherapy</u>, medication therapy, holistic therapy or a combination of these, as many as eighty percent or more improve dramatically. Unfortunately, many people with depression still suffer in silence, perhaps because they do not recognize the <u>symptoms of depression</u> or feel they cannot afford medical treatment for their disease.

- If you or someone you know suffers from depression make sure you get help. There are literally thousands of online and offline <u>support</u> organizations.

CHAPTER 7

Coming out of the Dark

Religion and spirituality are vital for survivors of any kind of trauma. Christianity was never pushed on me by my parents. In fact, I would consider myself to be a spiritual person, taking elements of faith from many different religions and applying them to my life. I identify as a Christian because I believe that Christ is the savior of man and died so that we may

all live. I grew up watching my grandmother, Minnie, pray heavily and she encouraged me to read the Bible early on in life in order to find answers to questions that I asked her about. To this day, I can talk to her about love, compassion and praying anytime day or night. I credit her with establishing a prayerful environment for my father during his childhood. His faith also played a key part in his recovery; I am allowing mine to let me heal as well. My pastor has also been in my life since I was 2 years old. She knows my accomplishments and my struggles so it is also easy for me to confide in her. Quite naturally, I spent a lot of my life questioning God. At 16, when best friend. Despite what anyone thinks or says about me I know that He loves me and that I am a good person.

I found comfort in the following verses: **The Lord is my strength and my praise: and he is become my salvation. (Psalms 118:14), Fear not, for I am with thee: turn not aside, for I am thy God: I have strengthened thee, and have helped thee, and the right hand of my**

His purpose for me may still not be clear but I know I am meant to tell my story. I am not a holy roller, nor do I attend church every Sunday. I party on Friday and Saturday but God knows my heart. I am no longer angry with God, my parents or myself. I haven't yet forgiven them but that is a work in progress. I found peace in knowing that my experiences happened for a reason.

CHAPTER **8**

Dance with my Father

My father's drinking was never obvious to me. He was always patient and soft spoken with me. To me he was everything and more. My father always filled our house with music, singing and dancing. From his stories I learned that my grandfather loved to dance and taught him, he continued that tradition with me. It was the one thing that allowed us to be free. When we danced and sang there was no pain, there was no fear. Pops had his instruments, turntables, maracas, drums, records and of course stereo system. You name the album and he had it and I thought that Michael Jackson would be my future husband. If it were a parallel universe maybe my brothers and I could have been like the Jacksons. Today, we are all involved in writing and the music business in some way and my father has everything to do with that. Despite all of the chaos he was able to establish an emphasis on Black culture, especially poetry and music in our household. There were carnivals, ice cream, jokes and making our own music videos. To me, life with Pops was perfect. That all changed as the arguing between my parents progressed into physical altercations. Who hit whom is a blur and I truthfully don't remember anything about these fights because I had begun to disassociate, step outside of myself from all of the trauma. One day when I was seven years old I sat on a pillow on my bed gazing out of the window. Pops told me that day that he had to leave. I could see the pain all over his face and I knew one day I would be able to forgive him. My teen years I thought about this day and became angry that my father would leave me with a woman he knew was mentally unstable. It was the ultimate selfish act and I felt like he did not fight for my brothers and me as hard as he had fought for himself. My parents split early on in my life, and then I didn't understand my Pops damn near sacrificed his own sanity for myself and my brothers. Now I know how it feels. He calls them "crazy makers"; people who will do anything to make you lose your mind. I suffered from Bulimia, depression, anxiety. My friends got me through. When I was younger I would write stories and plays to reflect my own childhood. The system had failed us; it heavily favored women back then so my father never stood a chance to win custody. Who would grant custody to an alcoholic anyway? Even when Pops left and Mitzy moved my brothers and I back to New York my youngest brother and I were able to spend the summers with Pops in Boston. I would attend AA meetings with him from the time that I was 6 years old. I had no idea the demons my father was dealing with. I saw him go from a halfway house to a room to an apartment, and now to a beautiful home. To me that is symbolic of his growth as a man and a father. 25 years later he is still clean and sober. He got sober for himself. Today, I realize that he got sober for his family as well. My relationship with my father is also still in progress. He kind of sprung a new family on me, although I know his intentions were not to hurt me or leave me out. I know that he is still trying to establish a sense of normalcy after all of these years. However, at times I can't help but to feel left out of his future and feel like a part of a past that he is trying to forget. Like I said, I did not ask my parents to make me or choose to be here, none of us did. Pops has never directly harmed me in thought, word, action or deed but like many Black females I still struggle with him not being in my life consistently. I can only hope time will continue to heal our relationship and I can forgive him as well. I love Pops and I know I can talk to him about anything because we are both natural counselors. When he got his coin for 25 years sober in AA I made a speech I had not even prepared in advance. I had really just come to be supportive and show him that I was proud of him. I know that God spoke through me that day, I was finally able to put into words what I felt all of those years. Anyone who has an addict for a parent knows that it is an internal battle for them and all you can really do is be there to cheer them on. Pops is an excellent example of someone who did the work to get sober and he inspires me every day. I know our bond is greater than the recent rifts that we have had and I am blessed that I know my father. Hell, I see his face every day when I look in the mirror, the man spit me out. Pops is the first man I ever loved and I can't wait for the day when I find someone like him to show me the unconditional love that he has.

CHAPTER 9

One Step at a Time

I look back, 11 years later and see that girl and I don't know her. I thank my parents for that. They made me a fighter. I was a latch key kid, which means they didn't raise me at all. My brothers did, and then a pedophile took over. I am strong because of what I have overcome. I love them for that. I hate them for all the lies, trauma and drama. I know how not to raise my children, especially a daughter. She will fly, not crawl like I did for years. I am walking right now with God on my right. Life isn't perfect now just like it wasn't then but I am living. I have always aspired to change the lives of young people. I believe that I already have just by living on my own accord. We all are survivors; I thank Mitzy for the tough love, life lessons and for making me a fighter. There's nothing I can't beat because of her. Some days it seemed like my siblings and I were given this life for a reason. Other days, I thought God just didn't love us or had forgotten about us. This book is for every little brown girl going through hell right now and every little brown boy screaming for attention. Going to jail, fighting in gangs, making babies; that's how we cry out. It's time to shout in a different way, stop taking things of the past on like a suit of armor that will only weigh us down. The past can no longer predict the future. We have to make it; follow God's plan for us. I am not telling you all of this to feel sorry for me or to feel better about your own lives. I am telling my story to inspire. I want every young Black woman to know that life brings adversity and pain but you can be triumphant. What God brings us to He brings us through.

There is no storm too great for you. So put on your galoshes and hold up that umbrella because it's going to be a bumpy ride but you will make it through, I know you will. I did and the sunshine after is all worth it.

CHAPTER 10

Flying without Wings

Writing has been my way of dealing with the pain. I now see a creative arts therapist in the Bronx who encourages me to not only deal with the past but have hope for the future. I am able to express myself through different kinds of art. I am an artist by birth but how my emotions correlate with it is something I have never explored. I thank her for allowing me to break through the layers of emotional walls so that I can one day find my true self again. I strongly recommend therapy to everyone, not because I am now the daughter of a therapist but because I think it is important for people to talk about their issues and life in general, especially in times like these. It doesn't mean that you are "crazy" or that something is "wrong ". The only crazy thing is recognizing that you need help and not doing anything about it.

I almost gave up on this life at a very young age. When I see the news and read about teen suicides I am able to not only sympathize and feel sad like most people but also know exactly what it's like to feel like that is the only way out. My first book was comprised of poems that I had authored during my greatest depressions in life. I wanted to show that there can be light even when you are in the darkest of places. It was not that successful but I felt pride in knowing that I could change someone's mind about themselves with words. Self-encouragement is the only way a woman can survive in society. Everyone will tell you what you can't do but it is up to you to determine that you can do anything and then go ahead and do it! Many of my English and Creative Writing teachers never fostered my talent; I was even denied entry into Honors English in high school. I let a lot of things knock me down but I never let anything keep me there! A fire has been ignited in me since turning 30 earlier this year. I live simply for the fact that I love life. What I went through does not define me. It is not who I am or will be. My old self has died and I have been reborn. I love freely and know that God will give me everything I need and more in time as long as I continue to work hard for it. I started to write short stories after my poetry book was published. I decided to share an excerpt of one of the first ones I had written, titled "On the Wings of Angels".

"On the Wings of Angels"

Raven sat up in her bed; her feet dangled over the side close to the top of the bed. She kneeled by the side of the bed and began to pray. "God its Raven-I know I ask this all the time but please let today be the day daddy stops drinking and Mitzy gets better." I promise I'll be good forever." Every day she repeats the same prayer at the start of her day, hoping that the night before that this so called life would somehow get better just by putting those words out into the universe.

Somehow inspired by the sunlight pouring into her room by the single window Raven hops out of her kneeling position and up into a cartwheel. Despite the horrors she faced every day, her demeanor remained childlike and playful. Raven was ready for the day, She peered open her bedroom window slowly and looked out down the long hallway that separated her bedroom from the upstairs bathroom. There seemed to be no one in sight. As she swung on the banister leading to the bathroom she saw shattered glass sprawled out on the living room floor. Hearing her mother's voice in her head she ran back into her bedroom and threw on her Bugs Bunny slippers.

She crept down the stairs and inspected the glass first from afar and then with her hands.

It was so shiny and translucent. She held a tiny piece up to the sunlight peered out of a window trying to see the world in a different way. Instead her mother's reflection peered back at her Raven jumped and threw the glass to the floor.

"Girl what the hell are you doing?!" her mother shouted. "Why would you pick up glass dummy don't you know you can get cut?" She watched as her mother swung open the closet door and pulled out the broom and dustpan. She swept with such vigor and thrust that she felt like she would fly away on the broom handle. The broken glass was flung with such force into the trash Raven was shaking like a leaf. "Mommy can I help you?" She asked.

Her mom turned around with that crooked smile that made Raven cringe. She knew something wasn't right about her mama when she smiled like that." What was that?" she said. "Can you help me? You know how you can help me—stay out of my way! "Raven ran back upstairs to her room and threw herself on the bed crying uncontrollably. About ten minutes later Raven heard a shuffling coming up the stairs, it was her mom. She quietly entered Raven's room and sat on the bed next to her. "Ladybug, I'm sorry for yelling at you" her mom sang as if she were a different person than the lady that just verbally assaulted her a few short moments ago. Raven looked up confused but lovingly wrapped her tiny arms around her mother's waist. "Mommy do you love me? She asked. "Well of course I do, her mother responded. I just don't like it when you do dumb things and when you make me mad. You know how momma gets when you make her made don't you?" She asked wide-eyed. Raven did not know if she should feel fear or relief that she was not screaming at her for once. Her mother crept out. Again, Raven knelt by the bed and prayed. "Dear God, please let tomorrow be a better day, Amen."

I have learned more from life in 30 short years then many twice my age ever will. It has given me more adversity than some may have been able to handle. At times, I get consumed with the thought of having a tragic life. But really, there was nothing tragic about my life. In every storm, God was my shield, my umbrella. The pain was good for me. I did not have a jaded view of the world and I know that shit can get real out here. I did not let myself go into the whirl wind of a life time of addiction, prostitution or go completely insane. If I did any of these things, any rational person would understand why but I wouldn't. That is not what God put me here for. Whether his intent was for me to go through the hell that I did, I will never know. It took many years for me to get over my anger at Him. Why did he let this happen? Where was He when I cried out to Him? Why didn't He send someone to help me? And simply, why me? What was it about me that He thought was so great, so special that I could overcome all of these things and still come out bruised but not broken? All of these questions are not answered. Maybe they are not meant for me to know the answers to. I do know that my spirit is intact and I may have not completely healed but I regret none of what was given to me and I made the best of it. I choose to end my story here but the pages are still being written. I hope that my story gave you hope. I pray that it inspires and teaches you that anything is possible. Where I come from is not where I have to remain. My circumstances won't determine who I am. My struggles have not been completely been overcome but I have broken the chains of abuse, and the truth is finally out. I no longer have to suffer in silence and neither do any of you who are or who have gone through it. Today, I am finally free. I am flying without wings. The pieces of my life that were shattered and scattered have been picked up one by one. One day I will finally be whole again and I can look above and thank God for showing me His grace.

Family over everything!

CHAPTER **11**

Back To My Roots

In December 2016, I abandoned Christianity, the only belief system I had ever known. I briefly dated a Muslim man and converted to Islam. I found peace, clarity and a connection to my ancestors through this religion.

I listened to Louis Farrakhan speeches daily, I attended 5 percent nation meetings in Brooklyn and really tried to find some spiritual connection and reason to all the events that had happened in my life. I did not know that the answer lay within me the whole time.

Much of our history is hidden in this country as Black Americans. One night in early January 2017 I dreamt of waves crashing and woke up in covered in sweat and short of breath. I thought it to be nothing more than the anxiety attacks I had become accustomed to, but this felt like so much more. I googled African Gods and Goddesses and stumbled upon information about Yemaya. From there I learned about the many other Orishas. I had a reading 6 years ago but never thought anything of it . TheShaman Priest had mentioned words being unwritten, it just dawned on me that was the title of my last book, my greatest success as an independent writer. I identify with Iya, Oya, Yemaya, Oshun the most. I see qualities of all of the goddesses in myself. My lifelong friend, who I refer to as my work mom, Pearl recommended a book to me called "The Accidental Santera" by Irene Itzo. I got chills so many times that I am still trying to complete this book. I was well aware that my family members possessed spiritual gifts under the guise of being "Christians". I think my great grandmother would be proud that I am revealing who we truly are. When I saw her photograph I can see in her eyes that she was an oracle, a healer, a miracle worker and the stories I have been told confirmed that. One of my favorite classes at the University was "Traditions of Storytelling". We lack that art now as Native, Indigenous and Black people. It was vital to our existence to know that slavery did not exactly happen as it is written in United States history books. You have to remember that this is not a country but a corporation that serves the purpose of White, privileged individuals. We were never meant to survive the pillaging of our land, rape of our woman or the systematic mind control of oppression. Once you go to the ancestors in spirit, they will reveal your gifts and your true selves. I do not identify as a Muslim, a Christian or a person that practices Santeria. I believe in spiritual warfare, lessons, teachings, the realization of our gifts as natives to this land. I will never be blind enough to sit in anyone's church again, that is the religion of my oppressor. Since I have tapped into my roots, I have grown stronger than ever, like a tree planted by still water.

There is nothing around me but peace and no one can take that from me because I now know who I am. The power we possess as Indigenous women has been lost because of poor diet, lack of exercise, lack of knowledge and lack of support by the men in our communities who mostly do not know themselves either. Being Creole and Ethiopian, Irish and Native American can be confusing to the spirit but I have learned which part of me to tap into to reach my full potential.

The "G" Chapter

One night, a summer night in 2001, Pops and I had a really bad argument. He did not and still to this day does not know how to deal with me when I am angry. He promptly told me to "get my Black ass in the car". He was driving so fast that I did not know where I was going nor did I think I wanted to go. We rolled up to a strange looking building outside of Boston. It was in the middle of the woods, very intimidating and creepy for 19 year old me to see given the childhood trauma I had already experienced. I walked in and sat with an older White man with a beard and glasses. It turns out he was the intake counselor for the group home we had pulled up to. I was completely checked out, fidgeting and twitching trying my best to stay awake at that point. He asked me a series of standard questions and I answered dryly. I walked up some clunky wooden stairs with him. His lean frame carried him slightly into the banister as he held the railing and assured me that I was safe and everything was going to be ok.

He gestured for me to take the far bed, the only unoccupied one. There in the bunks lay two other girls. One of the girls, Mary, was a pretty Latina with jet Black hair. She immediately sat up upon seeing me. The other girl, a heavy set Black girl, Rose also opened her eyes, peered up at me and sat straight up. I stood there awkwardly as I always do when it's time to meet new people. (I have what psychologists call a "slow to warm up" personality). Mary swung her legs off the bunk and walked up to me looking me up and down. The counselor walked downstairs and said "ok girls, have a good night. " Mary unlocked her gaze from me and walked back to her bed. "So, who violated you?" was her first question. I lifted my head and just barely whispered back in response," Mr. B". "Pieces of Shit!" she replied back. This, of course, broke the silence and she and I both laughed. Rose then sat up and said "Well I was lucky both parents did me." My face fell in absolute horror. I walked over to my bed and took off my shoes to get comfortable-I was with my tribe.

Rose and Mary helped me get toiletries together from the cabinet in the morning. Breakfast was at 7:45am, the food was pretty good there. I had scrambled eggs, wheat toast with butter and hot tea with lemon. They watched me eat and then we walked up those clunky steps where I was led to the bathroom.

Rose pointed up to a white wash cloth that was soaked with blood. "No, this is the one you use" she instructed me. I looked at her bewildered and said "what do you mean?" Everyone who knows me knows I have OCD (Obsessive Compulsive Disorder) so I was not wrapping my head around what she was saying at all. She repeated, "This is the one you use". I cringed and Mary chimed in, "We want to protect you. We don't want anyone to hurt you again, ever." It was then that I realized what she meant. She was a Blood, I was about to become one too by association. I have always been around "the life". People may assume that growing up in the suburbs I had no inkling of anything outside of the perfectly manicured lawns and nice homes that I grew up surrounded by. My parents relocated to the suburbs from the projects of Yonkers, NY as you recall, early on in my life. I do, however, remember our roots, the things I saw in my childhood definitely weren't cookie cutter.

I am aware that being associated didn't mean I had to run around with colors on or hurt anyone, I was simply always protected.

Everywhere I went the next couple of days, Rose and Mary were right next to me. We bonded, laughed, did craft, watched movies, did each other's hair and of course ate all meals together. At night we would trade stories of our experiences with abuse. When I told mine, they both were wide –eyed and attentive so I knew I would write this book someday. Pops picked me up at the end of that week. I learned a lot about myself, others who didn't have a parent or living parent that cared about them. Researching gangs and gang culture for another upcoming book of mine, I came to find out via urban dictionary.com (don't judge me) that "G" doesn't stand just for gangster or gangster as we have all come to know.

A "G" doesn't necessarily refer to a gangster. In Queens, among the individuals I'm acquainted with, a "G" is basically a person who has their "shit together"....or someone who is good at life, all around. An individual who is good looking, in good shape, is intelligent, has money, is good with people, is with hot women, is well dressed etc. is a "G." Therefore, the majority of the hip-hop/gangster community are not G's at all due to their lack of brains, money, social skill, class, style etc. (Source: www.urbandictionary.com).

The original origins of gang culture also do not include the interpretations that the younger generations have included today.

Here is where it would be good for me to say, "Never judge a book by its cover".

After 36 years of life I can conclude that I am nowhere near being required to having it all figured out. I have made a considerable small fortune after my first book release, 'The Fading Rainbow". My ex stole the royalties from that and 4 years ago I was once again scammed by an ex who wrote checks in my name to over 20 women. I have been wealthy, offered wealth by men, dirt poor, lived in my car, apartments and with roommates. I am aware of every perspective of this life. I have chosen spirituality, as the saying goes, "religion is for people who believe in hell and spirituality is for those who have already been there".

This book is for 8 year old me and for all the little Black Girls who smile despite the heart ache and Black boys filled with joy although the world assumes and hates them.

We are a strong people. Our bloodline dictates that we survive. Thank you to all of you that have been along on my journey so far; it continues!

I never met you but I've heard so much about you. This page is for my great grandparents. You instilled strong Christian values in all of your children. Because of you both none of us are afraid of a little hard work! Our family tree continues to grow and I know you are both looking down from heaven smiling, proud of all of my family members. Our family bond can never be broken, we are strong united, weak divided.

Printed in the United States
By Bookmasters